IMAGES
of America

ELGIN

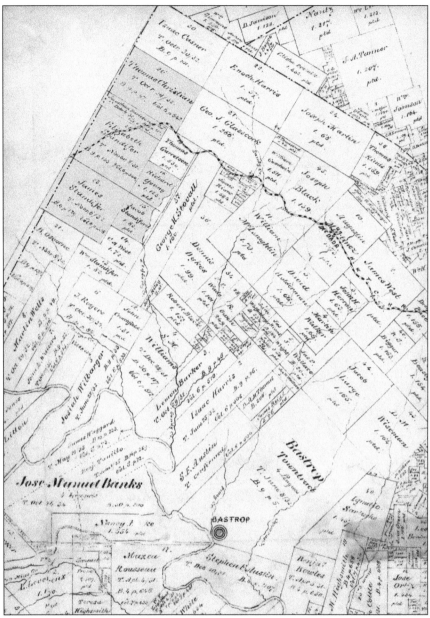

EARLY LAND GRANTS. In 1832, the northern boundary of Stephen F. Austin's "Little Colony" followed the current boundaries of Bastrop County, and a system developed concerning allocation of land. A married man with a family could receive 4,428 acres, but a single man could only receive 1,107 acres. The Mexican government required no money for the land, only a promise to pay $6 in taxes after five years. (Courtesy of Elgin Depot Museum.)

ON THE COVER: A SATURDAY IN ELGIN. In 1914, wagons crowded Main Street, and Elgin's population doubled each Saturday when all the farmers and their families came to town to trade, visit, and buy supplies. The ladies window-shopped for the latest fashions and housewares, the children played tag up and down the blocks, and the men talked crops. Everyone looked forward to Saturdays in Elgin. (Courtesy of Elgin Depot Museum.)

IMAGES
of America

ELGIN

Sydna Davis Arbuckle
Judy Davis

ARCADIA
PUBLISHING

Published by Arcadia Publishing
Charleston, South Carolina

Library of Congress Control Number: 2012949678

For all general information, please contact Arcadia Publishing:
Telephone 843-853-2070
Fax 843-853-0044
E-mail sales@arcadiapublishing.com
For customer service and orders:
Toll-Free 1-888-313-2665

Visit us on the Internet at www.arcadiapublishing.com

*This volume is dedicated to our mother, Nell Been Davis.
She had a great love for documenting events and people that
paved the way in her life. She instilled this love in us.*

CONTENTS

ACKNOWLEDGMENTS

This book would have never come to fruition without the efforts of Ann Helgeson, factotum of the Elgin Depot Museum. A native of Iowa, she has lived on four different continents but has since settled in Elgin, becoming the foremost expert on Elgin history. Thank you, Ann. Elgin owes you a great debt of gratitude!

All pictures, except where noted, are from the very large and extensive photograph archives of the Elgin Depot Museum.

INTRODUCTION

Elgin owes its existence to a flood. In the late 1860s, the Houston & Texas Central (H&TC) Railroad surveyed Bastrop County with the plan of extending the railroad from Brenham to Austin with the proposed routing going as close to the Colorado River as possible in order to service the cotton plantations near Webberville. Nature had other plans though. The great flood of 1869 completely submerged the proposed railroad bed, and a new plan was adopted to route the rails through present-day Elgin and Manor to Austin. The H&TC had contracted to reach Austin by January 1, 1872, and the line, built mainly with convict labor, was completed a few days ahead of schedule. On Christmas Day 1871, the first train steamed through what is now Elgin and arrived in Austin ahead of the contract deadline.

But the history of Elgin goes back to 1832 to Stephen F. Austin's "Little Colony," when Thomas Christian and Jonathan Burleson, both members of Austin's colony, received land grants from the Mexican government. These two grants were north of the new town of Bastrop, and Elgin now sits on a portion of each of these grants.

In 1872, Theodore Kosse of the H&TC platted the Elgin townsite, as he did many other towns along the railroad. The town was named after Robert Morris Elgin, land commissioners for the H&TC. Robert Elgin agreed to lend his name to this new town as long as it retained the proper Scottish pronunciation with a "hard g," as in the word "begin."

Two and a half miles to the south of the new railhead of Elgin lay the thriving community of Perryville, nicknamed Hogeye, but the post office there was officially named Young's Settlement. No wonder history can be confusing. The people of Perryville began moving to Elgin when they recognized business opportunities because of the railroad. A growth spurt ensued, and a hotel was built, several stores opened for business, a saloon provided spirits to the new community, and a doctor opened his office along with a drugstore. Lots were sold, families settled close to the railroad, and churches and schools were established in the community.

Spiritual strength for the new community came from the churches that were organized. Some of the earliest denominations were Baptist, Methodist, Christian, and Presbyterian congregations. German and Swedes were instrumental in forming Lutheran churches in the area, and the Catholic Church served most of the Mexican community.

The young village recognized the importance of education and the first school bell rang in 1874 for 172 children. Three teachers imparted knowledge to the students who were charged $1- to $2-per-month tuition. In 1879, Elgin High School, a private institution, held its first session, and a teacher deemed "a thorough knowledge of the subject matter will be necessary for a broad and full mental culture." The private school continued to be the chief means of education until the Texas school law implemented the community school system in order for the parents to organize into free school communities and share in the benefits of the available state school funds. The Elgin Independent School District did not come into being until 1897. Three separate—but equal —school systems were organized: one for the white students, one for the black students, and one for the Mexican students. In hindsight, they were anything but equal. Full integration did not arrive in Elgin until 1969.

Most of the commerce in Elgin's early days came from farming. West of town was the rich black soil that grew cotton, corn, and feed crops. East of town was sandy soil that produced the finest watermelons, cantaloupes, sweet potatoes, peanuts, tomatoes, and a host of truck crops. Immigrants from Germany, Sweden, Czechoslovakia, and Mexico arrived in great numbers when word of Elgin's temperate climate reached them. Many freed slaves lived in the area, and others migrated to the area after Emancipation because of the fertile land and job opportunities.

As different nationalities moved into Elgin, they brought their customs, languages, and religions with them. Thomas O'Connor moved to Elgin in the late 1800s to build brick cisterns, wells, and fireplaces. He obtained his bricks from the Butler plant in Austin but soon discovered a promising bed of clay in the Elgin area. In 1882, he began making bricks by hand, using wooden molds and drying them in the sun. Several buildings in Elgin made from these handpressed bricks are still in use. Other brick-makers realized the opportunities with the rich clay, and the brick-making industry was established and is still the leading industry of Elgin.

Elgin's cotton crops demanded processing and rapid transportation to markets throughout the United States. The railroad provided the shipping capabilities, and steam-powered cotton gins were plentiful in the 1870s. A gin could process 8 to 10 bales a day, but the advent of diesel power in 1917 increased the number to 50 to 60 bales a day.

Newspaper publishing was one of the early businesses in Elgin's formative years. The *Elgin Meteor* began publishing in 1879, followed by the *Elgin Times* in 1882. The *Elgin Courier* ("*Courier*") was established in 1890 and is still in business today. Old copies of the *Courier* are full of priceless historical information about Elgin. The Elgin Historical Association has a project photographing the old *Couriers*, page by page, preserving the information on CDs .

The World War II years saw a spike in Elgin's population because of Camp Swift, a large Army camp that was constructed midway between Elgin and Bastrop. The camp was activated in 1942 and was the training center for 44,000 men at one point. Servicemen's dependents flocked to Elgin for lodging, and every available room, closet, and shed was rented during the war years. In 1943, Camp Swift received its first group of prisoners of war (POWs) who had been captured in Tunisia and were members of the elite Afrika Corps of the German army. More than 3,000 POWs were housed at Camp Swift, and many worked outside the camp for local farmers or at the Elgin brick plants. The POWs were sent back in 1946, but most wanted to stay in the United States because they had been treated fairly and saw no future in returning to a defeated land. Camp Swift was deactivated in 1947. Departure of the military was a blow to Elgin's economy.

Many events have added to Elgin's history since the end of Camp Swift, but we try to document here, through pictures and narratives, a time that many never knew—the century from 1860 to 1960. Even though Elgin's population today hovers around 10,000, we still retain the small-town atmosphere that is attractive to those seeking an escape from large city traffic, pollution, and crowds.

One

FROM HOGEYE TO ELGIN

Elgin's history began at Young's Settlement, a small community located about 2.5 miles south of the site of present Elgin. It was established on land that had been granted to Elizabeth Standifer in 1829 as part of the Stephen F. Austin "Little Colony." Fierce Indians roamed and controlled the area until after the Texas Revolution, when Michael Young and his family settled in the most northern portion of Bastrop County. The village was also known as Perryville or Hogeye.

At one time in the 1850s or 1860s, Young's Settlement served as a stage stop and had a saloon, a general store, two blacksmith shops, a grocery, and 12 to 15 households. One unusual business venture, begun shortly after the Civil War, used camels as freight carriers. Bethel Coopwood and Enon Lanfear bought 32 "US Government Surplus" camels and attempted to use them to carry mail and other items between San Antonio, Brownsville, and Mexico City. The business failed because the camels could not operate in the rocky soils of Texas.

In late 1871, the H&TC completed a contract to connect Brenham to Austin by rail, thus bypassing Young's Settlement by approximately two miles. Soon, residents began moving their homes and businesses toward the railroad and what would become the city of Elgin.

The post office at Young's Settlement was discontinued at the end of 1872, and the new settlement of Elgin gained a post office in April 1873. The initial application for the Elgin Post Office stated that it would serve a population of 250, and the town of Elgin was incorporated on May 31, 1873.

MARY CHRISTIAN BURLESON HOME.
Thomas Christian and Jonathan Burleson each received land grants in 1832 on which Elgin is situated. Christian was killed in the Wilbarger scalping incident, and Mary Christian later married James Burleson, the father of Jonathan Burleson. Because of fierce Indian attacks, the Burleson family lived in Bastrop until they built the pictured house in 1847 in the Elgin area. The house is still standing in 2012, and plans are being formulated to restore it to its original condition.

MICHAEL YOUNG. Michael Young and his wife, Rachel, came to Texas from Alabama in 1829 and settled in Fort Bend County. Young fought in the battles of Anahuac and San Jacinto. He moved his family to the Indian-infested northern part of Bastrop County in 1838. Many relatives from Alabama and Tennessee later followed him to Texas and became the first residents of Young's Settlement. (Courtesy of Ruth Crowson.)

JOHN LITTON'S TOMBSTONE. John Litton married Sarah Standifer, Elizabeth Standifer's daughter, and their home at Young's Settlement not only served as an inn and a stage stop but also housed the first post office. John Litton was a veteran of San Jacinto and the first postmaster. Originally buried at Young's Settlement, his body was moved to the state cemetery in the 1936 Texas Centennial recognition.

MABLE LITTON CONDRON AT LITTON INN. Mable Litton Condron is shown at her grandparents' inn at Young's Settlement, which was the stage stand for the Concord stages. This stop became known as Hogeye because of a community dance that once was held and the lone musician, a fiddler, knew only one tune, called "Hogeye," which he played over and over as the crowd danced.

11

MEEKS LOG CABIN. The sparsely populated area known as Young's Settlement or Hogeye was extensive, reaching from the Travis County line to Wilbarger Creek and to Old Sayers Road. This house, built in 1851, was originally known as the "Meeks Cabin at Hogeye." It was acquired by the Rivers family, became a home of C.B. and Mary Lucy Rivers Maynard, and is now known as the Sweet Lucy Ranch.

WILLIAM BAILEY STANDIFER HOME. William Bailey Standifer, the son of Elizabeth Standifer, fought in the Battle of San Jacinto and is buried in a family cemetery off of Monkey Road. Standifer was a farmer and lived in the Young's Settlement area from 1838 until his death in 1878. His daughter Martha Standifer Arbuckle is shown in front of the family home in Hogeye.

JANE BELL, FORMER SLAVE.
Young's Settlement voted against
secession from the Union, yet
offered aid as Texas supported
the Confederacy. In 1865, when
the slaves of Bastrop County
were freed, some remained
working for former owners;
others started businesses and
purchased land of their own.
The Bell family purchased land
between Young's Settlement
and Utley. Jane was the
matriarch of the family, which
is still active in area affairs.

**OLD BAPTIST CEMETERY
(PERRYVILLE).** Young's
Settlement became the official
name when it was granted a
post office in 1849. However,
many knew the community as
Perryville in honor of Michael
Young's son Perry, while others
familiarly called it Hogeye
because of the dance at the
Litton Inn. The churches and
Masonic lodge carried the name
of Perryville. The Perryville
Baptist Cemetery is located
in the area of Farm-to-Market
Road 1704 and Beaver Road.

1879 RAILROAD MAP. The H&TC completed its line from Houston to Austin with an alternative route because of a flood in 1869. The initial plan closely followed the Colorado River to avail the Webberville cotton farmers a way to get product to market. Because the proposed way was flooded, an alternate route via Manor was chosen, and a watering station was created 2.5 miles north of Hogeye.

CONVICT LABOR. The railroad was largely built by convict labor, using wheelbarrows and mules to build up much of the dirt work. Miles Hill, the founder of the *Elgin Courier*, wrote that he had many times "seen convicts in stocks, as punishment for their failure to do the work demanded of them."

FIRST TRAIN THROUGH ELGIN AREA. The H&TC fulfilled its contract to connect Houston and Austin by rail by 1872. The Austin paper reported the following: "On Christmas Day, 1871, the railroad came to Austin. True, it was not on time, and the gay throngs, bands, and welcoming officials had dispersed in the rain before it actually arrived. A whole week of excursions and balls followed this momentous occasion." (Courtesy of Austin History Center.)

ROBERT MORRISS ELGIN. The H&TC Railroad created the town of Elgin on August 18, 1872, and named the new point on its line for Robert Morriss Elgin, the railroad's land commissioner. Although Elgin never lived in his namesake town, he lent his name with one caveat—"Pronounce my name correctly!" The Scottish pronunciation is used with a "hard g," like in "begin." Elginites continue to correct mispronunciations!

MILES SALOON. Commerce developed near the railroad in the new town, and residents and laborers wanted their liquor. The Miles Saloon opened in 1872; soon there were six others in town until 1913, when Elgin voted to go dry. Mr. A. Christian operated one of the early saloons and his sign indicated "A. Christian Saloon." A restored sign on the original building is still a topic of conversation when viewed today.

A BED AND HOT MEAL. Boardinghouses were in much demand in the new town. In 1876, Sallie McDonald operated this place at the intersection of the present North Avenue C and West Second Street. Her husband ran a livery stable on the south side of the railroad tracks.

REST FOR THE WEARY.
Elgin's first hotel, the Joplin, was on Main Street. Train arrivals were greeted by a fiddler singing, "Calhoun's Saloon and Standifer's Street, Joplin's Hotel and nothing to eat." The pictured hotel, also known as the Meeks Hotel, was built in 1880. It was a two-story building, painted green, and located on Depot Street facing the H&TC track. The Meeks Hotel and adjacent businesses were destroyed by fire in October 1898.

JOHN GORDON'S TOMBSTONE.
John Gordon, the first station agent and telegrapher for the H&TC railroad in Elgin, died in 1882. His wife purchased a lot for $200 from the H&TC railroad to use for his burial. She later sold the lot to the City of Elgin for $200 for use as the city cemetery. (Note the telegrapher's key engraved on the stone.)

ELGIN'S FIRST POST OFFICE. Edward Smithwick was appointed the first postmaster in 1873 and the post office occupied a portion of the newly erected Grange Building. It later moved three times prior to the present post office building, which was constructed in 1939. In 1912, Elgin was chosen the first town in Texas with a population of under 5,000 to begin a new experiment for free home delivery service.

WAITING FOR PRESIDENT MCKINLEY. Tension ran high in Texas after the Civil War. To set an example of reconciliation, Pres. William McKinley, a former Union officer, came to Austin in 1901 to visit with Gov. Joseph Sayers, a former Confederate veteran. President McKinley then went to Houston, and his train passed through Elgin. The picture shows the people of Elgin in 1901 waiting for the presidential train.

EARLY SOUTHSIDE BUSINESSES. The town of Elgin incorporated as the city of Elgin on September 12, 1901. Charles Gillespie was elected the first mayor. Others elected were J.D. Hemphill as marshal and W.E. McCullough, J. Wed Davis, Ed Lawhon, Max Hirsh, and F.S. Wade as aldermen. The first ordinance passed by the city government prohibited trains proceeding beyond the speed of 10 miles per hour through the city or they would be fined $100.

GENERAL STORES. Early general stores in Elgin took care of their customers. Not only did they offer merchandise that could feed, clothe, and supply most family needs, but also the stores had wagon yards at the rear of their businesses where farmers and their families could come from the rural areas to shop, visit, and camp overnight.

19

RAILROAD HANDCAR. The railroads used hand-propelled cars to inspect and maintain the rails. These cars carried tools and were light enough that they could be lifted off the tracks for passing trains. Earl Eggleston and Lottie Krueger are pictured on an afternoon date, and the photograph could have been used as their engagement picture.

H&TC SECTION HOUSE. The railroad companies divided the tracks into sections between 10 and 30 miles long and assigned a foreman and crew to tend each section. The company usually supplied a house near the tracks for the foreman and his family. The pictured H&TC section house and toolshed were built in 1884 near the Oil Mill and continued in operation until the mid-1950s.

UNION DEPOT. The Missouri, Kansas & Texas Railroad ("KATY") built a line in 1886 joining Taylor, Elgin, and Bastrop. Elgin was now at the junction of the KATY and H&TC (later Southern Pacific) railroads. In 1903, the red brick station was built for Elgin passengers and was known as a Union depot because it was jointly owned by the two railroads. For many years, four-day and four-night passenger trains stopped at Elgin. In 1924, it was agreed that the KATY would operate and maintain the depot. This arrangement ensued until 1954, when passenger service ended. In 1959, the City of Elgin purchased the depot building for $2,000 and used the building as its police department and jail until 1993. Finally, in 2002, the restored Union Depot opened as the Elgin Depot Museum, and it serves as a showplace for information about Elgin's past.

21

TELEPHONES. By 1900, Elgin was served by two competing telephone companies. The Independent Telephone Company and Southwestern Bell Telephone Company ("Bell") both served businesses and residents, making it necessary for many to have two instruments to adequately be available for all. From left to right, Estelle Casey, Irene Barker, and Susie Taylor are shown at the Bell switchboard. Bell purchased their competition in 1925 and exclusively served Elgin until the 1980s.

WATER. In 1905, Elgin was considered the fastest-growing town in the United States, and people were demanding utilities. Water from wells at Carr Springs, five miles east of town, was piped to the city. The initial water system, consisting of a wire-wrapped wood pipe with wooden collars and lines, was laid in ditches and turned with an oversized road plow, as shown by Albert M. Clopton's road crew. Elgin at last had running water by 1909.

ELECTRICITY. Elgin's first electrical plant, as shown, opened in 1901. Poles were erected, and service agreements were signed according to "drops" in a house. Wallace Webb related in his oral history that his father, Judge C.W. Webb, signed on for two drops—drops of electrical cord for a light in two different rooms in his house.

ICE DELIVERY. Ice was a commodity that changed food preparation, and people purchased wooden iceboxes with tin ice storage chambers to store food. With the availability of electricity, Elgin had two ice plants by 1910 that could produce 9 to 10 tons of ice daily and provide a place for cold storage. This unidentified wagon driver delivered ice in 50-pound blocks to residents every day except Sunday.

MAIN STREET IN 1908. Elgin had become a thriving business and agricultural center in its 36 years of existence. The main street was home to a variety of buildings and businesses, and a good cotton crop made life easier for the area farmers. News of this new thriving area brought settlers from Sweden, Germany, and Mexico to the area, and the Elgin store clerks were fluent in Swedish, German, and Spanish.

BASSIST OPERA HOUSE. Elgin boasted of two "theaters" where lectures, local talent, and traveling vaudeville shows were presented. The Bassist Opera House was built in 1906 by Phillip Bassist, a Jewish immigrant from Germany. The ground floor housed a grocery store, and the post office was in the back portion. A staircase went up to the opera house.

SKATING RINK. Tents provided a place for entertainment, whether it be skating, Chautauqua lectures, dog and pony shows, or medicine shows. The corner of Main Street and Lexington Road was a popular tent site, and William Jennings Bryan once appeared here for the Chautauquas.

VETERANS' PARK. Veterans' Park was established in 1913 when the ladies of the New Century Club signed a lease with the railroad for the right-of-way land, which had been occupied by a lumberyard. The railroad assisted the ladies in their plans for the park with sidewalks, shrubs, trees, and a bandstand. The park became a gathering place for many city functions and is still the focal point of downtown activities.

SAM J. SMITH HOME. By 1907, Elgin had a population of more than 2,000, and large homes were being built within the area. Sam Smith married Sara Christian, the daughter of Mary Christian Burleson, and the Smiths built their home near the present Sunset Motel.

NOFSINGER HOUSE. Dr. I.B. Nofsinger practiced medicine in McDade before coming to Elgin. In 1906, he constructed his home on Main Street; it is used today as city hall. Dr. Nofsinger's wife, Mary, was a registered pharmacist and operated the Reliable Drug Company while he carried on his medical practice.

TRAVELING HOME. Dr. T.B. Taylor (pictured with his buggy and unidentified children) had a large house in Paige. When he moved his medical practice to Elgin, he dismantled the house in Paige and rebuilt it in Elgin, near Avenue B and West First Street. In 1908, Dr. Taylor bought some lots and decided to move the house to a location near North Main and Eleventh Streets. The project took over a month and was done by using a winch hooked to a post in the middle of the street. The family lived in the house while it was in transit to its new location. Several years later, Dr. Taylor decided to move his practice to Bastrop and he had the house dismantled again and rebuilt almost in its original architecture in Bastrop. It still can be seen in Bastrop today.

W.H. Rivers Home. W.H. "Bud" Rivers built his family home in 1900, located between Elgin and Hogeye. Rivers began clerking in Elgin in 1876 for $15 a month and made it a practice to save one-third of everything earned. In 1881, he married Lucy J. Owens, and they were the parents of four sons and two daughters. Pictured are, from left to right, (first row) Mary, W.H. "Bud," Ruth, Lucy J., and Roy; (second row) Leon, Howard, and Wayland. Bud Rivers was a great benefactor to the Elgin area; he opened a mercantile establishment, set up a private bank, amassed much farmland, and helped set up the educational system in Elgin. He was the president of the Elgin National Bank, the First National Bank of Thorndale, and the Texas Bankers Association. Descendants of this early family are still active in the civic and economic growth of Elgin.

Two

Street Scenes with Business and Industry

With the railroad well established in the late 1800s, commerce and industry came to Elgin because of the ease of shipping and receiving goods for the growing town. Deep beds of clay made Elgin the "brick capital of the southwest," and the rich, cotton-producing soil made agriculture to one of the top-producing industries of the area. It was only natural that banking played an important role in Elgin's development.

From the early days of Thomas O'Connor making bricks by hand and drying them in the sun to the most modern brick-manufacturing equipment today, Elgin has long been known for its fine-quality masonry products that have been used throughout the Western Hemisphere. Elgin presently has three major brick manufacturing plants, but the bricks are shipped out on trucks now since the rail companies no longer serve Elgin.

The fertile blackland soil to the west of Elgin was perfect for cotton production, and the first cotton gin began operation in 1878. At one point, there were eight gins operating in and around Elgin in order to keep up with the cotton harvests. Cotton is still grown on the "prairie," but there are no local gins today. However, the Elgin Oil Mill still processes the cottonseeds and turns them into oil and fertilizer and cattle feed. As early as 1908, J.O. Smith, editor of the *Elgin Courier*, warned farmers not to rely on one crop. He encouraged them to focus also on the by-products of the farm, like poultry, butter, milk, cattle, and pork. Farmers listened, and Elgin soon began shipping these products by rail on the 10 trains serving Elgin daily.

Today, Elginites still farm and produce bricks, but many commute to nearby Austin for jobs in technology and state government.

Hanke's Gin. In 1878, Silas Chatfield built the first cotton gin–gristmill–sawmill in Elgin, and it was later sold to the Henry Hanke family in 1883. The gin produced 10 bales of cotton a day when Hanke bought the steam outfit, and when the modern electric gin closed in 1970, it was producing 60 bales a day. As many as eight gins operated in the Elgin area during the heyday of King Cotton.

A Bumper Crop. Some early cotton gins produced both square and round bales. A square bale weighed 500 pounds, and a round bale weighed 200 pounds. By 1890, the railroads in Elgin provided transportation for easy shipping to large markets. Imagine Elgin's pride when Elginite Sadie Martin McCullough studied cotton classing in Houston, came home, and became the first woman cotton-buyer in Texas.

ELGIN COTTON OIL MILL. The Elgin Cotton Oil Mill opened in 1906 in response to the bountiful cotton crops produced around the area. Farmers could locally sell the by-products of seeds and hulls. E.O. Lundgren Sr. became manager after World War I and eventually became the owner. This mill is still operated by the Lundgren family and is one of four mills in the state.

THE *ELGIN COURIER*. Even though the *Elgin Courier* has provided community news for over 120 years, it was not the first newspaper in Elgin. The *Meteor*, the *Times*, the *Leader*, and the *Texas Bladet* (a Swedish paper) enjoyed short-lived fame prior to 1890. J.O. Smith, who bought the paper in 1901, operated the *Courier* for 46 years and also served seven terms in the Texas House of Representatives, representing Bastrop County.

ELGIN NATIONAL BANK. W.H. "Bud" Rivers opened a private bank in 1891. It was later incorporated as the Elgin National Bank in 1908. This bank, first located on the south side, moved to its present North Main Street location in 1923. The bank has changed names several times and is now Prosperity Bank of Elgin. The Rivers family directed and held the majority of stock until the latter part of the 20th century.

MERCHANTS AND FARMERS BANK. When the Merchants and Farmers Bank was organized in 1908, local people referred to this as the "Swedish Bank" because the officers and directors had Swedish surnames. The interior of the bank is shown with unidentified staff members and customers. Located in the two-story red brick building on the corner of North Main and West First Streets, it later became the Elgin State Bank, but all services were discontinued in 1939.

N.P. Smith Photography Studio. Swedish immigrant Nils P. Smith recorded Elgin history through his pictures between 1900 and 1950. Located on Main Street, the studio contained many photographic props and a large skylight for natural lighting prior to flash equipment. Many pictures in this book were taken by Smith or his nephew Bernhart Smith, who bought the studio from Nils when he retired and moved to Austin.

Make a House a Home. O'Connor Furniture Company began in 1884 in the pictured building that Thomas O'Connor built with his own handpressed and dried brick. Furniture, heating equipment, caskets, flooring, and kitchen appliances were available to customers. Three generations of O'Connors manned the store for over 85 years in the original building at the corner of Depot Street and North Avenue C.

FIRST TRADE EXCURSION. In 1910, automobiles began showing up on the dirt roads in the town and country. With faster rural transportation, Elgin became the hub for services and supplies. During the summer of 1917, these unidentified Elgin businessmen and a local band formed a caravan to visit all the communities in the area. The first week they visited the area south and

west of town; the second week they went to the area east and north. McDade, Fair Oaks, PeLee, Beaukiss, Siloam, Young's Prairie, Lawhon, Kimbro, Lund, Type, and other communities were excited to have these visitors! "Buy in Elgin" has long been the emphasis!

ELGIN SAUSAGE. The Texas State Legislature has designated Elgin the "Sausage Capital of Texas." In 1886, William Moon opened Southside Market, the oldest barbecue joint in Texas, parallel to the railroad track. Before refrigeration, meat markets had to sell or smoke meat before it spoiled. In true German tradition, Mr. Moon ground his beef trimmings, added salt and spices, and the original Elgin sausage was born. Below, an unidentified customer is shown in the old Southside location with, from left to right, Bud Frazier, Leo Maas, and Lee Wilson behind the meat counter. Progressing through several market owners, locals affectionately called the sausage delicacy "hot guts." Competition began after World War II when Hermina and Rudolph Meyer opened a small drive-in grocery, where they sold sausage made from their German family recipe. This competition continues through today, and town people still argue about which sausage is better—Southside's or Meyer's.

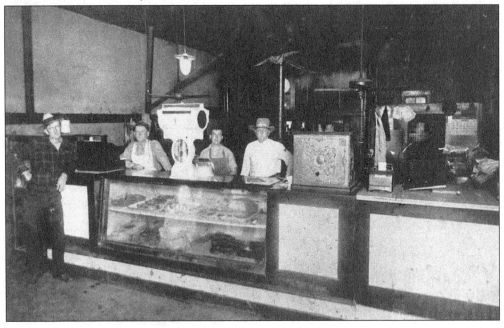

BRICK. Known as the "Brick Capital of the Southwest," brick manufacturing has been a major industry in Elgin since 1882, when Thomas O'Connor found rich red clay near Hanke Gin and began making bricks by hand. The Elgin Press Brick Co. began operations in 1897, and the Lasher Brick Company operated from 1906 to 1912. Unidentified workers are pictured as they remove fired brick from the kilns. The new century ushered in Butler Brick and Elgin Standard (Prewitt) Brick Company. Jobs for skilled and unskilled labor soon attracted workers from Elgin, and as far away as Mexico, because Butler and Prewitt both provided housing, a company store, and recreational facilities for the employees and their families. Today, those perks are gone, but the three nationally known brick plants still in the Elgin area are Butler, Acme (originally Prewitt), and Hanson.

MCCLELLAN INN. Tom Pfeiffer built the McClellan Inn across the tracks from the Elgin Depot in 1908 from timbers of the destroyed *Ben Hur*, an Austin pleasure boat. Upon completion of the 22-room building, the hotel was leased to Ethel McClellan. Traveling salesmen loved to dine and stay here and train passengers would telegraph lunch and dinner orders from Manor for their 20-minute stop in Elgin. The inn burned in 1952.

RELIABLE DRUGSTORE. Dr. I.B. Nofsinger began his medical practice in Elgin in 1906, and his wife, Mary McWilliams, was a pharmacist in their Reliable Drugstore, shown here. According to oral history, Dr. Nofsinger was upset when grocers sold patent medicine, so he bought barrels of sugar to sell at his drugstore to show the grocery merchants that two could play that game.

RIVERS BROS. MERCANTILE COMPANY. The brick building on South Main, adjacent to the original Elgin National Bank, was built in 1881 and housed the Rivers and Gresham Store. Later known as the Rivers and Carter Store, it became the Rivers Bros. Mercantile Company in 1905. Unidentified employees are pictured. The large upper floor of the building, known as Rivers Hall, served as a venue for meetings, parties, dances, and skating.

WE HAVE IT. According to this 1908 advertisement in the *Elgin Courier*, Rivers Bros. had everything one needed "from the cradle to the coffin." From plows to pillows and silk stockings to shrouds, it provided for home, farmers' needs, and wives' wishes.

CARTER & SANDERS GROCERY. Open flour bins in grocery stores were enticements for rodents. Wallace Webb related in his oral history that in 1911 he was employed to stop by his uncle Telly Sanders's store on his way to and from school to trap rats that inhabited the bins. He earned 5¢ a rat and averaged eight to ten rats a day. Maybe the unidentified boys in this picture are in line to apply for Webb's job!

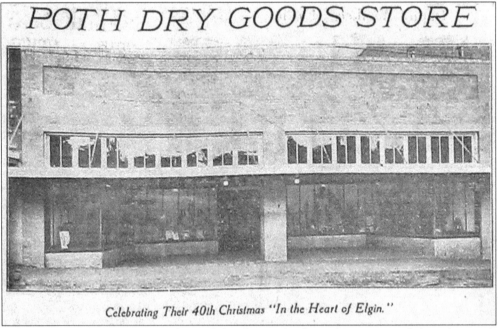

Celebrating Their 40th Christmas "In the Heart of Elgin."

FOR ELGIN'S FASHION-MINDED. The Poth brothers, Charles and E.B., opened their dry goods store in 1904, outfitting entire families for as little as $45. Charles admitted he did not know the difference between "calico and domestic" but he learned fast, and the store soon became the hallmark for fashion. The store was open on Main Street from 1904 to 1954.

LOOK AT MY NEW WHEELS. Men never change. They are always trying to impress young ladies with their new cars, and "dragging Main" was popular even in 1912. This group of unidentified sporting young Elgin men posed in front of John Puckett's garage on Main Street. John Puckett was one of the first car dealers in Elgin and sold Overland vehicles.

AUTOMOBILES COME TO ELGIN. Even though it looks as if everyone in Elgin owned a car, not many people did. Robert Johnson in 1920 had a thriving car rental business with a fleet of Model Ts, which he rented to young men who wanted to take their sweethearts for a Sunday afternoon drive in the countryside.

IF I HAD A HAMMER. Mutual Lumber Company catered to the needs of fast-growing Elgin by providing lumber and building supplies for local carpenters. Originally located on railroad property where Veterans' Park now stands, it moved to its longtime location at the corner of West First Street and Avenue C in 1914.

THE VILLAGE BLACKSMITH. Blacksmiths were necessary in early Elgin. They repaired farm equipment, kitchen utensils, made and sharpened knives, and kept carriages and wagons in fine running order. C.A. Burke opened this blacksmith shop in 1906. He and his son soon added a second floor to the building for woodworking purposes. Three generations of Burke men labored here from 1906 to 1957.

SHAVE AND A HAIRCUT. Elgin had several men's barbershops, but Ray's Barbershop outlasted all the others. People shown are, from left to right, Roy Ray, unidentified customer, Dermott Ray, unidentified customer, and Collis B. Taylor. Dermott Ray cut hair into his late 90s and in his oral history that men came to the shop on Sunday mornings for their weekly bath and shave prior to attending church. Barbershops provided entertainment, gossip, and hygiene.

THE PAUSE THAT REFRESHED ELGIN. Jake Hanson and son opened the City Bottling Works in 1906 and created and bottled carbonated beverages in seven different flavors. Successive owners made "Popkola," an Elgin favorite until 1942, when the pictured final owner, William B. Foehner, was drafted. He sold his business, located in the A. Christian Saloon building, to the 7-Up Bottling Company of Austin for its sugar allowance during World War II rationing.

MAIN STREET LIGHTS. Illumination of Elgin's Main Street in the 1920s was from lamps in the middle of the street. These lamps gave light and beauty to the town and greatly aided drivers with the ability to make U-turns. Elgin drivers today carry on this practice even though the lamps have been gone for 70 years.

FIRST FOR ELGIN. In 1925, A.E. Johnson opened a new filling station and garage, with the filling station operated by a woman, Jessie Bostic. A.E. Johnson took care of servicing the cars in his "up-to-date" garage and repair department in the rear. Johnson was an expert mechanic, machinist, blacksmith, and high-powered salesman, selling gas, oil, tires, and accessories. He is shown ready to deliver gasoline to his farm customers.

Q&S GROCERY AND MARKET. Oscar Swenson and Louis Lundgren purchased Q&S in 1925 and operated the business until 1977. Swenson (second from the left) and Lundgren (second from the right) are shown here with two unidentified employees. Q&S stood for quality and service, which were found there. The original location on Main Street burned in 1948, and a new building was built at North Main and Taylor Road.

ELI ARONSON IN 1934. For more than 30 years, Eli Aronson and his wife, Laverne, operated Aronson's Grocery on Main Street and offered exceptional personal service. One could shop the crowded aisles or order via telephone, monthly charge accounts were available with no interest, groceries were carried to the waiting cars or delivered to homes' kitchens at no charge, and the local gardeners had a market for their products.

FILL 'ER UP. By the 1930s, Elgin depended on several gasoline service stations and garages to keep their cars running. Anti-knox gasoline was selling for 15¢ a gallon, and Paul Farris was charging $5.69 for a Firestone tire. But it was a special Magnolia Service Station that provided an indoor restroom for ladies.

FLEMING HOSPITAL. Elgin has had many physicians over the years, but it was Dr. Joe V. Fleming who designed and built Fleming Hospital and opened it for patients in 1938. Following his untimely death in 1950, the name was changed to Fleming Memorial Hospital and operated under the leadership of Dr. Roy H. Morris Jr. until 1978, when the hospital closed.

Three

EDUCATION

Texas adopted a bill initiating public school education in 1871, but there was no permanent plans for implementation. Parents attempted to teach children at home or paid tuition to send students to private schools.

The new town of Elgin struggled with educating the young people. For the first 20 years, the town attempted to operate a community school in different homes or buildings. At the end of each school year, this community school was dissolved, and it was necessary to organize again the next year. There were no grade classifications, and the only method the teachers knew was to hear pupils recite their lessons individually. Simultaneous classroom instruction was still an innovation, and grading was unknown.

After one failed attempt, W.H. "Bud" Rivers led Elgin in 1897 to incorporate an independent school district that was comprised of four square miles of area. Rivers, the largest tax payer in the district, contended it was "cheaper and much more charitable to pay taxes to erect buildings in which to educate the children than it was to pay taxes to build penitentiaries." The district was approved, and a second election levied a tax rate of 50¢ on 100 valuations to issue $9,000 in bonds for erecting a school. This tax-approval election received a unanimous vote! The Elgin Independent School District (Elgin ISD) opened the first school building in 1898 and served the district until 1954. In 1910, the 11th grade was added to the standard education curriculum for Texas, Elgin built a second building on the north side of town, compulsory attendance was initiated in 1915, and the state began providing textbooks in 1918. In 2012, the district contains 168 square miles in portions of Bastrop, Lee, and Travis Counties and has a total enrollment of 4,041 students with 241 teachers spread across six campuses. Approximately 45 percent of the students live outside the city limits of Elgin. In 2014, a campus of Austin Community College is scheduled to open in Elgin, giving the opportunity for Elgin students to obtain education beyond the high school level and compete in the job markets of the 21st century.

FIRST SCHOOL IN ELGIN. Records indicate that the first school in Elgin was taught by A.H. Carter in 1874 for 172 students at the present site of the original Masonic lodge location on Avenue B. The school was supported by subscriptions and tuition—the usual tuition fee being $1 or $2 per child per month. The picture, taken in 1891, is the first school picture that could be found.

MRS. KEEBLE'S SCHOOL. Many parents chose to send their children to private schools operated by churches or individuals. Mrs. M.B. Keeble operated a school in the back of her residence on the corner of Avenue A and Central Avenue. This 1898 patriotic pageant photograph featured unidentified costumed students with W.H. Rivers Jr. standing in front wearing the tri-corn hat.

48

LOWER GRADES, 1897. Maude Campbell is shown here with the last class she taught in the school that met in the Masonic lodge location. The next year, Maude Campbell, Miss Goldsmith, and Mrs. McMullen taught the first six grades in the new red brick south school.

SCHOOL FOR GERMAN CHILDREN. Immigrants from Germany wanted their children to speak English and excel in subjects. The German citizens hired Professor Bolle to teach pupils during the summer terms of 1898 and 1899 at the Avenue B lodge location.

THE RED BRICK SOUTH SCHOOL. Elgin's first permanent school building opened on September 5, 1898, with 200 students. This eight-classroom building, with a library, cloakrooms, and book closets, housed grades one through ten. The first graduating class from Elgin High School in 1900 was composed of three students. The building housed different levels of classes from 1898 through 1954.

THE NORTH SCHOOL. By 1910, the South School was so crowded that students were attending a half-day schedule. Elgin built this new building facing Avenue H between Beaukiss Lane and East Sixth Street. Soon, the South School became the grammar school for the first through seventh grades, and the North School housed the high school until 1927. Subjects taught in high school included Latin, German, trigonometry, science, and domestic economics.

BEACON STAFF OF 1916. As shown here, various unidentified students of Elgin High School have published remembrance albums since 1914 through the present day. The annuals have carried three names through the years: the *Beacon* was the first annual; the next one was the *Wildcat*; the third one was the *Cat's Paw*. The name has since reverted back to the *Wildcat*.

ELGIN MEXICAN SCHOOL, 1917. Elgin rented a residence to house a separate Mexican school until 1921. The 1908 *Courier* carried the announcement that "the pupils have made wonderful advancements. There were only two boys that could speak English and they could only speak a few words at the beginning. The pupils can now read, write . . . cipher in arithmetic through multiplication. Nearly all read through their third readers."

ELGIN GRAMMAR SCHOOL, 1922. Through 24 years of use, the South School had evolved from the only building in the Elgin ISD system to the school for the elementary grades. Simple playground equipment had been installed, the ladies of the town ensured an inside restroom was installed in 1918, and an outside building was provided as a lunch room, where lunches were furnished by private homes or students brought their sack lunches. Students were required to be seven years

of age (the compulsory school age of six was adopted in 1923) and show proof of a smallpox vaccination to begin first grade. Classes started each day with a pledge to the American flag, and curriculum was divided between low and high grades; for example, a student could be in either low fourth grade or high fourth grade.

LAMAR SCHOOL. In 1921, the Lamar School, a separate Mexican two-room school, was built on Williams Street. Even though the school was separate, all classes were taught in English, and students were reprimanded or punished for speaking Spanish on the school grounds. This school was in operation for students with Hispanic surnames until 1947. (Courtesy of the University of Texas Libraries, the University of Texas at Austin.)

LAMAR SCHOOL PRIVY. In 1946, a picture of the Lamar Mexican School privy was used in a lawsuit to prove that the separate schools in Elgin were anything but equal. The lawsuit led to the abolition of separate Mexican schools in Texas, and in 1947, all Mexican students in Elgin began attending Elgin Elementary and Elgin High School. (Courtesy of the University of Texas Libraries, the University of Texas at Austin.)

WASHINGTON SCHOOL, 1925. Education of the Negro students in Elgin began in 1882 near the site of the Westbrook Cemetery. In 1891, the Little Flock Baptist Church organized a second school nearby to teach additional grades and subjects. By 1925, there were more than 150 students attending these schools, and a new building was erected on Houston Street. This school building was in use from 1925 until 1960, when a new brick building was constructed on South Avenue F. Prior to the mid-1950s, Washington teachers who wanted to take graduate courses spent summers out of state. No Texas Negro college had graduate programs, and segregation prevented local teachers from attending white-only colleges and universities. J.C. Madison served as principal of the Negro schools from 1914 until 1940. D.P. Johnson followed Madison and served from 1940 to 1967. Beginning in 1967, the Elgin ISD was completely integrated.

New Elgin High School, 1927. By 1925, the North School had been condemned for structural and sanitary reasons. After many town meetings, a location was chosen in the north part of town on North Avenue C. A two-story brick building in the shape of an "E" was constructed and opened in January 1927. The new school housed grades seven through 11. Enough land was acquired to later include athletic facilities. The school auditorium became the meeting place for the town for the next 50 years. When high school classes moved in 1976 to another location, this building continued to be used by the Elgin ISD and is now, after extensive refurbishing, the administration building.

VELMA LESEMAN'S CLASS IN 1933. In 1930, with the nation deep in the Depression, Elgin ISD determined it would not hire any married women as teachers. This was in force for four years. Velma Leseman was a spinster who taught three generations of first-grade students. Students often wondered if Velma could write cursive because she always printed!

KITTIE HENDERSON. Kittie Henderson was a longtime Elgin teacher who served in elementary, junior high, high school, and administrative positions. Her teaching span stretched from the 1920s through the 1960s. She was the great-granddaughter of Mary Christian Burleson, Elgin's first resident. Kittie Henderson traveled internationally during her summer vacations and inspired students to explore the world, either through books or travel.

NELL OWENS AND PRINCE. Another spinster teacher from one of Elgin's pioneering families, "Miss Nell" could often be seen riding her horse named Prince. When Prince would escape his confines, she would send some of her male students to round up the errant equine. Miss Nell, a graduate of the Elgin schools, taught elementary, junior high, and high school classes and even coached the tennis team.

BLANCHE ROBINSON. Blanche Robinson taught for many years at the Washington School. She is shown here with her elementary students, probably in the 1930s. Robinson taught several generations within families. Her daughter taught in Elgin, and she has two granddaughters currently on the faculty of Elgin ISD.

1915 Girls' Basketball Team. The Elgin ISD added an athletic program for physical training and competitive sports to the system's academic courses in 1910 for both girls and boys. The original school colors were brown and white. The 1915 Elgin girls' basketball team posed for a picture for the *Beacon* and the narrative indicated the following: "Played one game. Did not win, but worked hard."

Elgin's First Football Team, 1917. In his oral history, Wallace Webb describes Elgin's first football team and tells that each player got to choose his number. Lonnie Pfeiffer chose No. 9, and Paul Moore chose No. 1. None of the other players were identified, but Jack Standifer was listed as the team mascot.

TWO EARLY FOOTBALL PLAYERS. By 1920, the school was providing uniforms for the team that included these two unidentified football players. However, the team members had to pay 10¢ each to obtain the one ball for the season, and they had to pay their own way on the trains to out-of-town games. Local games were played at the ballpark off Central Avenue behind the Bethel Methodist Church.

SCHOOL FIRE ESCAPE. In the 1930s, laws were mandated for outdoor fire escapes to be added to multistoried schools, and the pictured fire escape was added outside the second story of the Elgin Grammar School. Former female students will never forget wearing dresses during fire drills and sailing down the hot slide with the splintered railings. (Courtesy of the University of Texas Libraries, the University of Texas at Austin.)

1935 FOOTBALL TEAM. The Great Depression extinguished many programs for the school from 1930 to 1935. In 1935, Elgin had a new superintendent, three busses were purchased to begin bus routes, football was reinstated, the "Wildcat" was chosen as the school mascot, and the school colors of purple and white were chosen. A lighted football field was set up behind the high school, and J.C. Koen (pictured) taught history and coached football.

ELGIN BAND, 1941. September 1941 found the 12th grade being added to all Texas schools, and students entering Elgin schools would now attend classes for 12 years. The Elgin High School Band was the pride of the town and it was truly unique. Seldom did one find a concert band that included an accordion!

1946 Washington High Eagles. Basketball was very popular, although gymnasiums did not exist for indoor games in Elgin since the North School was demolished. Some of the 1946 Washington High team members have descendants as stars for Elgin High basketball in 2012. Pictured are, from left to right, (second row) Martin McDonald, coach; Allen Harrell; T.J. Hicks; Alford Nash; H.P. Brown; Willie C. Harrell; (first row) A.J. Hammons; Bill Hibbs; and Clifford Brown.

Washington High School Band, 1953. Music was always an important part of life at Washington High, and high-stepping majorettes led the band at all football games. Band director Jesse Hart saw to it that students learned the basics of music and marching, and the group was a showpiece of precision and talent as they took to the field for halftime performances.

SENIOR TRIP, 1949. In the late 1940s through the early 1960s, an incentive to graduate was the bonus of going on the senior trip. The 1949 class traveled to New York and Washington, DC, and the students had their picture taken on the steps of the Capitol. The students traveled in a yellow school bus and spent nights in high school gymnasiums. Later, classes traveled by charter bus and stayed in hotels.

BUS BREAKS DOWN. The only mishap of the 28-day 1949 senior trip was when the fuel pump on the bus went out between Buffalo, New York, and New York City. Some of the boys hitchhiked into town to purchase a new pump, and class member Curtis Craig replaced it while Supt. C.E. Brown and sponsor Bernhart Smith looked on.

JUNIOR-SENIOR BANQUET. Elgin ISD built a gymnasium behind the high school in 1947. For years, the juniors honored the seniors with a dinner and dance in this gymnasium. Weeks were spent decorating, with crepe paper stretched across to change the atmosphere from athletics to exotic places. This was the predecessor to the current proms held out of town with students arriving in limousines.

GROUND BREAKING FOR ELGIN ELEMENTARY. The red brick school on South Avenue C had served the educational needs of Elgin from 1898 to 1954. Ground breaking in the spring of 1954 preceded the building of the new Elgin Elementary School by Davis Construction Company of Corpus Christi. Ben, Dale, and Mack Davis had all attended the red brick school in their youth and now built the new school in their hometown.

THE CINDERELLA TEAM OF 1958. Fielding a team of underweight, inexperienced boys who loved football in 1958, new head coach James Lyda saw something special in this group of ragtag players. After the first five games of the season, it looked as if it would be another ho-hum year for the Elgin team, but then momentum took over, and the Wildcats posted wins against larger and stronger teams. The *Austin American* called them the "Cinderella team" and predicted each week they would lose. Elgin came together as a community and shared the dream of winning the state championship. The scoreboard at the state championship game showed White Deer as the winner, but the team of 1958 gave Elgin an experience to remember, and the record still stands today as the longest football season in Elgin history.

BARRIER BROKEN. The Elgin athlete that history will best remember is John Hill Westbrook. Westbrook was the first black student to play varsity football in the Southwest Athletic Conference. Westbrook was a graduate of Elgin's Washington High School where he ran track, played basketball, and football and was salutatorian of his class. He played for Baylor University from 1966 through 1968 and had a too-brief career of service after graduation. He endured much to remove the stain of segregation from a conference that had not allowed blacks to participate in its activities. Westbrook died in 1983 of a blood clot in his lungs.

Four

SACRED AND SECULAR

Organizations based on beliefs, purposes, common interests, languages, historical heritages, and dreams have guided the Elgin community since early times.

Elgin drew many immigrants because of the adjoining rich farmland. Europeans arrived to a community where different ceremonies and church denominations existed. Not feeling comfortable in the local forms of worship, these people continued worshiping in the languages and rituals of their homelands, and Swedish and German churches dotted the countryside. These groups met socially to continue the customs, dances, and music and to encourage the children of these first-generation Americans.

Groups soon organized to give fire protection; others organized to create parks in the city; and some organized to perpetuate the remembrances of those fighting in wars. Secret organizations, with some exhibiting questionable purposes, also came to be. The women of Elgin banded together intent on intellectual advancement as well as social justice and they worked diligently to gain the right to vote for women.

Elgin was always a community to help, whether through organizations or individual efforts. Churches cooperated in citywide revivals, crops were gathered for neighbors, groups came together for "hog butcherings,' benefits were held for people when they lost their houses to fire, businesses closed for funerals, and "poundings" were held to help newlyweds.

And this trait continues today. Benefits are held for cancer patients, bank accounts are begun for children who have lost parents, people donate time and money to food banks, and the "Elgin Caregivers" drive senior citizens to doctor appointments all over Central Texas.

Working together, whether sacred or secular, Elgin is a caring community!

ELGIN FIRST UNITED METHODIST CHURCH. The Elgin Methodist Church was organized in 1874 with a weekly Sunday school and a monthly church service. Many of its members came from the Perryville Methodist and the Pleasant Grove Methodist congregations. In 1882, a one-room frame building was built on the site of the present sanctuary, and in 1905, the present sanctuary was built at a cost of $10,000. Beautiful memorial stained-glass windows and a pipe organ have been distinguishing features for over 100 years. The pictures show the church in 1907 (above) and its appearance as of 2000 (below).

FIRST BAPTIST CHURCH. John Gordon, the first station agent for the H&TC Railroad, organized a Baptist Sunday school in 1873, and the actual organization of a church took place in 1875. Many Perryville Baptist Church members transferred into the Elgin church, which also met in the Masonic lodge–school building on West Third Street. In 1884, the pictured frame church was built on the corner of North Avenue C and West Third Street. In 1923, the present sanctuary was built. The original plans called for the building to have a steeple, but a steeple was not added until 70 years later.

MOUNT MORIAH MISSIONARY BAPTIST CHURCH. Mount Moriah was organized in 1879 when Presley George of the Pleasant Grove Community gave a group of ex-slaves permission to build a place of worship on his property. The pictured church originally was located near the Westbrook Cemetery and was moved in 1901 into town. The church burned in 1938 and was soon rebuilt and used until 1960, when the present building was erected.

CHURCH OF CHRIST. Early history of the Church of Christ indicates the purchase of property on Old McDade Road in 1911. However, by 1921, the congregation was meeting in the Central Christian Church, later in the State Bank Building, and finally in the Presbyterian church on Sunday afternoons. The church pictured above, built on North Avenue C in 1932, was used until 1958, when it was replaced by the present building.

CENTRAL CHRISTIAN CHURCH. Members from the Christian Church at Young's Prairie moved into the town of Elgin, and in 1888, the Central Christian Church was organized. In 1892, the original structure was built, only to have it destroyed in the far-reaching 1900 Galveston storm. A second building was erected but was also destroyed by a storm in 1915. The structure was rebuilt in 1916, and this frame building was used until 1965, when the current one was built.

HAM-RAMSEY REVIVAL. Early Elgin churches cooperated in citywide revivals. In 1913, the evangelistic team of Rev. Mordecai Ham and singer W.J. Ramsey from Kentucky led a five-week revival at the skating rink, and it was a spiritual awakening for Elgin. Later in the 1930s, the Reverend Ham was preaching a revival in North Carolina, and a man named Billy Graham was converted.

GATHER AT THE RIVER. Public baptisms were held in creeks, rivers, and stock tanks for many Elgin churches. Immersion symbolized being buried to sin and rising to a new life in Christ and was necessary for joining some Christian churches. Many converts were baptized in the Colorado River in the 1920s.

NEW SWEDEN LUTHERAN CHURCH. Immigrants from Sweden began arriving about 1867 in eastern Travis County to the settlement of Knight's Ranch. The name was changed to New Sweden when the Swedish Lutheran Church was organized in 1877. People continued coming to the area six miles north of Elgin and built the church pictured at right in 1879. In 1911, the congregation built the present-day church pictured below, and this beautiful building has been seen in movies, been the subject of magazine articles, and is a landmark for remembrance of the Swedish pioneers.

ROSE HILL LUTHERAN CHOIR, 1910. Many people emigrated from Germany to the Elgin area. On July 14, 1918, the Elgin St. Peter's Evangelical Lutheran Church was organized; a frame building was purchased in 1924 and moved from the Rose Hill community near Manor. The two congregations merged and worshipped in this original building until the present edifice was built in 1953. The current bell that tolls is from Rose Hill.

ST. PETER'S LUTHERAN CHURCH. During the organizational years, St. Peter's congregation met in homes, the Union Railroad Station, and the Central Christian Church. Some sermons continued to be preached in German through the 1930s; services were held in this building until 1953.

SACRED HEART CATHOLIC
CHURCH. Many Mexican
immigrants who came to work
in the coal mines or brickyards
were Catholic. In 1911, a
mission church was organized
in Elgin and dedicated to the
Sacred Heart. Several years
later, members helped build
the church pictured above near
the corner of North Avenue
A and West Second Street.
In 1945, Mr. and Mrs. Albert
Mikulencak deeded some lots
on West Eleventh Street and a
chapel moved from Camp Swift
was the new home. The former
military chapel (pictured at
right) burned in 1955, and the
current building was erected
on the same site in 1957.

FIRST PRESBYTERIAN CHURCH. In 1881, Elgin Cumberland Presbyterian Church was organized, and in 1886, a small white frame structure for worship was built. Circuit riders and part-time pastors conducted services. In 1909, this congregation became the First Presbyterian Church USA of Elgin, and a red brick sanctuary that is still in use today was constructed.

GERMAN BAPTIST CHURCH. German people from the Greenvine area near Brenham moved to Elgin around 1910. Under the leadership of August Klaus and John Sipple, a German Baptist Church was organized in 1921. The congregation erected a building on North Avenue H at Sixth Street, and this church continued until 1949, when it dissolved and the membership transferred to the First Baptist Church.

EVANGELICAL FREE CHURCH.
Some immigrants left Sweden to
escape the state church. Swedish
groups organized the Swedish
Evangelical Free Church in
Kimbro in 1897 and the Swedish
Evangelical Free Church of Type
in 1908. The two small churches
worshiped independently until
1954, when they joined together
and organized a new Evangelical
Free Church in Elgin. The Kimbro
church building was moved
into town and is still in use.

ELGIN MASONIC LODGE. Organized
in 1870 and transferred from
Perryville, the Elgin Masonic
Lodge was the first secular
organization in Elgin. This secret
all-male organization stressed
education and helped widows and
orphans. Secrecy necessitated its
meeting rooms to be on second
floors or in buildings without
windows. This building, shared
with the *Elgin Courier*, was the
1897 meeting place; the present
Masonic Hall was built in 1965.

WOMEN'S POWER. Pictured here, the Elgin New Century Club was organized in 1897 by women who wanted to enlighten themselves through study and make Elgin a better place to live. These women forged ahead to develop Veterans' Park, pushed for women's suffrage, led the way for Prohibition in 1913, supervised public health programs, organized the first public library (below) in Elgin, and stayed connected to state and national politics. A building from Camp Swift was obtained as a clubhouse in 1948, and the club existed from the end of the 19th century into the beginning of the 21st century—more than 100 years.

KKK Funeral. In the early 1920s, Elgin had a large Ku Klux Klan membership, which wore white robes and hoods to meetings and ceremonies. This secret male vigilante organization instilled fear as they rallied against Negroes, foreigners, Jews, and Catholics and attempted to correct moral discrepancies. The picture shows a clan ritual at the burial of a member.

American Legion. Veterans returning after World War I founded the American Legion; the Elgin post was named to honor Elginite Henry A. Lundgren who was killed in action. Pictured are Laverne Lundgren Owens and E.O. "Sammy" Lundgren Jr. They beat the Elgin American Legion drum in 1928 for Uncle Sam and their Uncle Henry when the band performed at the 10th National American Legion convention in San Antonio.

ELGIN FIRE DEPARTMENT. Fire was an ever-present danger to young Elgin, and as early as 1897, there was a group of volunteer firemen whose equipment (pictured) was a cart with a reel and hose and a hook and ladder. After Elgin acquired its water system in 1909, fire hydrants were available to help in fighting fires, and mules pulled the fire wagons for the newly organized 1910 fire department. Bucket brigades were used frequently when the available hoses would not reach to the new fire hydrants. The area felt safer when the motorized fire engine seen below was purchased in 1916, and the mules were retired. A permanent two-story fire station was built in 1925 but was replaced with a new building in 1986 on the same location. In 2012, the all-volunteer Elgin Fire Department now numbers 40.

MEETINGS, MEETINGS, AND MORE MEETINGS. These announcements from the 1923 *Courier* show that people have always worked together for purposes of church, civic matters, personal interests, social reforms, and to accomplish goals. Elgin once had chapters of the Odd Fellows lodge (IOFF) with their women's organization of Rebekahs, Woodmen of the World with their women's organization of Woodmen Circle, United Daughters of the Confederacy, a women's choir group named the Harmony Club, Order of the Eastern Star, a rifle club for women, a canning club, a Needle Crafters Club, an Elgin orchestra, several elite 42 clubs, an association for truck-growers and hog-raisers, and the New Century Club. Community involvement precedes progress!

SOCIETY

THEATRE PARTY

Tuesday evening Mrs. Will Standifer entertained a number of friends with a theatre party. The picture "Only a Shop Girl," was on for the evening and was of the great interest to the ladies.

Those enjoying this delightful hospitality were Mesdames C. W. Webb, John Baker, G. T. King, T. B. Sanders, Virgil King, Pat Burns, W. H. Carter, Alex Moore, Jack Fowler, Ned Carter and Miss Jewel Meek.

C. W. WEBB HAS BIRTHDAY

Friday, the 28th of September, marked the 46th anniversary of the birth of Judge C. W. Webb, one of Elgin's most prominent citizens, and as a compliment to him Mrs. Webb surprised him with a sumptuous birthday dinner, consisting of fried chicken and all its accompanying dishes, to which some of his men friends were invited.

Among those invited and present were Hon. A. M. Felts, Messrs. Howard Rivers, Chas. Poth, Ed Fromme, Leon Rivers, R. Severn, J. O. Smith, Earl Strauss, Powell Culp, Dr. W. E. Duff, and Dr. E. B. Auler and the honoree, C. W. Webb.

At the conclusion of the meal cigars and cigarettes were passed and a pleasant half-hour was spent in interesting conversation.

BROTHERHOOD CLASS ENTERTAIN

The members of the Brotherhood class of the Methodist Sunday School entertained for their families and

friends very delightfully last Friday evening on the church lawn.

The Elgin orchestra, directed by Mr. Will D. Nichols, dispensed sweet music throughout the evening. During the early hours of the evening, the little tots present held sway, playing many merry games, with Bro. Long as leader.

Miss Eva Long then took charge, directing the older ones in an "Apron" game, a class in the Siamese language and a newspaper stunt, all of which was delightfully amusing. Refreshments of sandwiches, punch and ice cream were bountifully served.

O. F. F. CLUB ORGANIZED

Miss Nell Owens was hostess to the members of last year's Merry Maids Club and a number of invited guests at her home last Friday evening. Progressive anagrams and a candy contest were features of entertainment. Later, in business meeting, officers for the coming year were elected and the club, to be known as O. F. F., was organized. The officers are: Mary Jane Burleson, president; Lutie Ruth Carter, vice president; Leonora Keeble, secretary; Dorothy Todd, treasurer; Modene Griffin, reporter.

Dainty refreshments were served. Miss Burleson, in response to urgent requests, gave enjoyable readings. Those in attendance were: Marjorie Meeks, Irene Couch, Lutie Ruth Carter, Mary Burleson, Frances Gustafson, Alice Harper, Lillian Martinson, Ruth Posey, Rosalie Mast, Olive Jackson, Eloise Ramsey, Dorothy Todd, Maxine Hirsch, Mattie Maud Swayze, Zelma Prowitt, Ruby McCall, Leonora Keeble, Modene Griffin.

MATINEE 42 CLUB.

The pretty home of Mrs. Louis Diesch was the place of meeting of

the Matinee 42 Club Friday afternoon when they held their regular meeting. A color scheme of pink and green was charmingly carried out in the reception rooms, with floral touches of queens wreath and roses.

Five tables of players spent a most delightful afternoon, closing with the tenth game, following which, Mrs. Diesch, assisted by Mrs. L. M. Clopton, served dainty refreshments of chicken salad, sandwiches, olives, potato chips and iced tea. Plate favors were pink bon bon boxes filled with candy.

Two new members were welcomed at this meeting, Mesdames Allie George and C. W. Webb.

Those enjoying this delightful affair were: Mesdames J. M. Pucket, Ed Fromme, Joe Southernwood, Earl Strauss, W. H. Carter, Howard Rivers, W. E. Duff, A. M. Moore, T. B. Sanders, R. Severn, Edwin Hausler, C. W. Webb, Allie George, J. L. Burke, Leon Rivers, E. M. Salley, Ned Carter, L. M. Clopton, A. Z. Fullick, Pat Burns and Van Harris.

PICNIC FOR JUNIORS

Mesdames Chas. Carter and W. B. Keel and Miss Modene Griffin chaperoned the Junior Department of the Baptist Sunday School to Carter's park last Friday afternoon. After "playing wild", the children roasted wieners, toasted marshmallows, and enjoyed a picnic lunch.

O. E. S. NOTICE

The Eastern Star will hold Initiation Ceremonies Friday, October 6 1923, at 8 o'clock. Smithville Chapter will be our guests at this time. The entire membership is urged to be present.

Ever get tired building fires! Cole's Original Air Tight Wood Stoves hold the fire all night. Better look at one.   24-7

SONS OF HERMANN. Unidentified early members are shown of the Elgin chapter of the Sons of Hermann. The Elgin chapter was affiliated with the national lodge that had been formed in response to prejudice against German immigrants. The Germans of the area banded to face mutual problems and retain language, celebrations, and customs of their homeland.

SCANDINAVIAN CLUB. Descendants from Sweden and Denmark joined together through organizations to preserve pride in their heritage. In 1913, Esther Alquist, shown in a Swedish costume with her mother, Emely (left), and an unidentified woman, was in Skane, Sweden, to visit relatives. Esther was the mother of Emely Sundbeck, Leland Lundgren, and Karin Barker, and these three are still active in promoting Scandinavian pride.

Five

AGRICULTURE AND FARMING

Agriculture, including both farming and livestock production, has shaped the business scene of the Elgin area from its beginning. Rail transportation was available to convey products, and stores opened to provide services. Early citizens depended on agriculture whether by having a small garden and a family milk cow or claiming farming as a vocation.

The following excerpts from *Soil Survey of Bastrop County, Texas–1907* give an early description of the agriculture and farming practices in Bastrop County, including the Elgin area: "Bastrop County is an agricultural community having, however, a few industrial enterprises in coal mining, brick making, pottery and lumber . . . The greater part of the county's population is of comparatively recent citizenship and includes Americans, Germans, Swedes, Bohemians, Mexicans, and Negroes . . . The census of 1900 gives the average size of farms in the county as 110.9 acres."

Elgin met the challenge of the agricultural need for equipment and supplies. Blacksmith shops developed to forge plows and shoe horses, mule barns supplied animals to help with planting and harvesting, a feed and leather shop made saddles and repaired bridles and harnesses, a gristmill opened to grind corn meal and make flour, gins opened to gin the cotton, meat markets provided fresh meat from the local livestock, and an oil mill pressed oil from the cottonseed. All of these community businesses depended on agriculture.

In 2012, the business scene is completely changed, and the only agricultural businesses that have survived for over 100 years are the Elgin Cotton Oil Mill and Southside Market. Area farmers still produce some cotton, but the main crops are corn, milo, and wheat. The majority of the land is now pasture for livestock production; however, Elgin is still known for agricultural purposes. The Elgin Breeding Service is known throughout the world for its introduction and development of artificial insemination of cattle, and the Southwest Stallion Station is one of the nation's premier equine breeding and broodmare farms.

THE WESTBROOK FAMILY. After the Civil War, much of the Negro population of northern Bastrop County began to purchase its own farmland. Arthur Westbrook and his wife, Carolyn Scroggins Westbrook, were leaders in the black community. Carolyn was of mixed ancestry, being both black and Indian (from India). The Westbrooks had a two-story house in Elgin and owned 1,300 acres of land at one time. They were undertakers in the black community, had a dairy, and put milk on the train to send to Austin, Dallas, and Houston. The Westbrooks were members of the first black school and church. Arthur Westbrook and Carolyn are buried in the Pleasant Grove Cemetery alongside Arthur's white father, Bartholomew Westbrook.

EARLY FARMERS' MARKET. This July 1899 picture indicates this as the first exhibit of the Elgin Truck Growers Association. Truck farming is defined as hauling vegetables to market and selling directly to consumers without the help of middlemen or stores. Pictured here are squash, cabbage, potatoes, and other vegetables, as well as huge watermelons!

PABLO ROSAS. Mexican nationals began moving to the Elgin vicinity in 1907, hoping to find a better way of life. They found jobs on the farms, at the brickyards, and in coal mines near Bastrop. Pablo Rosas, pictured in 1912 with grandson Earnest and granddaughter Navarria, was one of the early settlers with a Mexican surname.

BAHN FARM. Wilhelm Bahn built his rock house, located south of Elgin, in 1887. He was one of the first of many residents with German ancestry. In 1900, one year before Spindletop, oil was discovered on this farm. Although there was never any production, Bahn had a constant source of equipment lubrication. This was the first of three times that "oil-patch hype" excited the Elgin community.

EXPERIMENTAL GASOLINE-POWERED TRACTOR. The Motor Plow Manufacturing Company was organized in 1910 to build one of the first experimental gasoline-powered tractors in Bastrop County on the Bahn farm south of Elgin. The pictured prototype with unidentified men was a product of typical German ingenuity and was financed by area citizens who bought shares at $25 each.

CZECH IMMIGRANTS. John Mogonye Sr. was a native of Czechoslovakia and served as a captain in the national army. He married Eva Dajka in 1878, and the couple (pictured) moved to the Elgin area in 1890. Through hard work using environmental practices and wise business decisions, Mogonye acquired land in Bastrop, Williamson, and Lee Counties, as well as a farm in central Mexico. Descendants of this couple today are still leaders in agricultural practices.

EARLY FARM EQUIPMENT. Immigrants came to the Elgin area, and many worked as tenant farmers until they could repay their passage and begin to purchase their own land. If the landowner furnished the land, the seed, similar tools to what is pictured, work stock, and a shack for the tenant, the owner received one half of the crop while the tenant did all the work.

HARVEST TIME. Hay was harvested when the grass dried. A horse-powered mowing machine had replaced the scythe for cutting, and horse-drawn rakes aided people in gathering and binding the hay into shocks. This picture confirms the fact that this process required work from all family members, hired laborers, and neighbors to gather enough hay to last through the winter.

GATHERING CORN. Corn was grown as a food product for humans, chickens, and livestock. Planting and harvesting methods did not change for centuries. Oscar Johnson is shown pulling corn by hand on his farm near Elgin. There was no waste of corn—the ears were eaten, the stalks were fed to cattle, and even the corncobs were a necessary item in the outdoor privies.

COTTON. Cotton was the chief cash crop in the beginning of the 20th century. The soil and weather conditions were advantageous for a profitable crop after much work. Mules pulled plows for planting and cultivating, and gathering was done by hand. They year 1908 was a bumper year, as shown with Joe King (left) and Max Hirsch (right) standing beside a train loaded with Elgin cotton. However, a great crop could not be expected every year. The boll weevil was a constant threat; it had entered Texas from Mexico at Brownsville in 1892 and gradually crept northward until 1900, when the weevils were blown all over Central Texas with the Galveston hurricane.

WEIGHING COTTON IN FIELDS. Cotton pickers were paid by the number of pounds they picked. The average wage in 1906 was 50¢ to 75¢ per 100 pounds picked. The sacks were weighed in the field prior to being dumped into a wagon, and a field hand kept record for each person and their earnings for the day.

HAULING COTTON FROM RIVERS FARM. W.H. "Bud" Rivers was the first entrepreneur of the Elgin area. Not only did he own a mercantile store and a bank on the south side of town but also raised much cotton on his land holdings in Central Texas.

PUCKETT'S GIN. After the cotton was picked, it was taken to one of the gins in the area. As pictured, Puckett's Gin was built in Elgin in 1912 and was run by steam. It burned in 1924 and was replaced by a new one in 1925. The new electric gin operated until the early 1950s.

COTTON FIELDS. Hannibal Lokumbe (Marvin Peterson), born in Smithville in 1949, is a jazz trumpeter and composer. He memorialized thoughts of his grandparents in his oratorio *African Portraits*. This symphonic composition includes a pleading spiritual known as *How Long*. The correct name for this spiritual is *Victor Carlson's Cotton Fields, Elgin, TX, 1940*. Lyrics include the following: "Lord, give me a sign of your heavenly grace . . . How long, sweet Jesus, how long?"

HARVESTING—A FAMILY OCCUPATION. Entire families from Elgin traveled to harvest cotton and vegetables in the Texas Panhandle and Northern states. All family members were expected to work, whether young or old. Children of the Rangel family from Elgin are shown picking cotton. Often, itinerant children returned home and entered school in November, only to have continual problems with studies because they missed so much schooling.

BUSY SOUTH SIDE. This 1912 street scene shows farmers with cotton bales on their wagons heading home to store the bales in their fields until the price was higher or taking them to the Elgin Cotton Yard to sell and transport by rail. M.L. Rivers's black horse is shown in the forefront with the Elgin Steam Laundry and Roy Rivers's Mule Barn across the street.

FARMING AT KIMBRO. In 1912, Ossian Carlson, a new immigrant, sent this picture as a postcard to his brother Oscar Carlson in Sweden. Oscar soon followed his brother Ossian to Texas and raised his family in the Elgin area. Likewise, many people from Sweden followed relatives to Central Texas and became some of the best farmers in Texas.

KYLBERG FAMILY TRACTOR. A.B. Kylberg shows off his Clytrac tractor in 1924 with unidentified family members. Tractors first appeared in the 1890s and were steam powered; gasoline-powered tractors emerged around 1910. The main job of the tractor was to pull equipment such as plows, shredders, rakes, and trailers. The Cleveland Tractor Company developed its tractor with track-type movements that did not get stuck as easily as the usual iron wheels.

EATING WATERMELON IN THE FIELD. The sandy soil east of Elgin was very favorable for growing watermelons. Trainloads of Elgin melons would be shipped in July to points all over the United States. These unidentified people are testimony that nothing would taste better than breaking a melon open in the field and devouring the sweet contents.

CHICKENS. Nearly every family, whether in town or country, had chickens in a pen. The chickens provided eggs and a source of meat. On Saturday afternoons, the squawking of chickens could be heard when a chicken was caught to have its neck wrung. The headless bird was then dressed, which meant it was plucked, cleaned of its innards, and cut into serving pieces. Sunday dinner usually featured a big platter of homegrown fried chicken!

FAMILY MILK COW. Most households always had a family cow to supply milk. The S.B. Oden family claimed that Daisy, shown here, gave 3.5 gallons of milk a day. Family chores included milking both in the morning and late afternoon. After taking a nursing calf away from its mother, the cow might continue providing milk for four or five years before drying up.

COUNTRY STORES. Most farming communities had a country store where gasoline for farm equipment, kerosene for cooking and lighting, nails, wire, and basic kitchen staples could be purchased without coming into Elgin but once a week. None of these stores exist today, but many farm children can remember going for a cold drink (a carbonated bottled drink) at their country store. Some may remember the Lund Store pictured above.

BEAUKISS STORE. Beaukiss, 15 miles northeast of Elgin, received its unusual name when it was granted a post office in the 1870s. The initial requested name was refused, and the Post Office Department asked for something distinctive about the area. Col. F.S. Wade replied, "At dusk you find buggies in every lane with beaus kissing their sweethearts." This caught the imagination in Washington, thus the name Beaukiss, Texas.

MANDA STORE. Otto Bengston operated this store in Manda with the post office being located in the front portion. This Swedish community was granted a post office in 1893 and was named Manda in honor of Bengston's sister Amanda. Much community pride developed around these farming locales.

TYPE STORE. Mr. and Mrs. William Schiller and Shirley Ann Anderson are pictured in front of the Type Store in 1939. Type, a crossroads community on Dry Brushy Creek, is located approximately five miles north of Elgin and was settled in the early 1900s by Swedish immigrants.

NEW SWEDEN STORE. The pictured New Sweden store now only exists in people's memories. The community is recognized today because of the beautiful church that remains and the cemetery that contains headstones with the names and dates of pioneer Swedes.

PE LEE NEWS

By Mrs. Lou Jensen.

PE LEE, Jan. 22—This snow affords a fine opportunity for cheap ice cream! We are sure enjoying to see the flakes coming down. But the freeze did quite a lot of damage here, Mr. Ed. Warren had a fine winter garden that was a complete loss. Mr. H. N. Smith figures over one hundred dollars damage by losing a fine radish crop. Some of A. N. Jensen's potatoes froze in one of the dryers. The cold coming on so sudden and with such a gale it is a wonder that people lived through it as well as they did. The thermometer fell from 65 to 18 in less than 15 hours, and later, Jan. 18, it dropped to 10 degrees. No report of death of any livestock here, for which we are thankful.

Mr. and Mrs. A. J. Jensen were invited to the Kramer home for ice-cream last Friday.

Mr. F. C. Smith and family called at the Jensen home last Sunday.

Several of the men went to the woods to earn missionary money chopping wood last Sunday and the ladies fixed up a bountiful dinner and brought it to them. We had a big fire to eat by and all seemed to enjoy a winter picnic. We had planned for all the church to go and educate the young folks on how to chop and saw wood but it proved to be too cold. Little Joan Jenkens and the writer were the smallest girls there I think.

We are sure real heartsore—Next Wednesday is my birthday and Mr. R. N. Jensen and his wife's twentieth anniversary and then R. N. was called to Bastrop on jury and his wife has to take the load of produce to Austin. And we had planned for a big feast. And even Mrs. N. K. Neilson has the same birthday, the first person I have ever met with that was born on Jan. 24 and I am the first one she has ever heard of. I just have a big notion to spread me two slices of bread with butter and fill it with onions and go and have dinner with her just to spite those Bastrop folk. They won't even let him beg off. Anyway, we were invited to H. N. Smith's for a good dinner last Sabbath, just me and my husband.

Mr. J. B. Hackworth spent last Friday evening at the Jensen home, just in time for ice cream!

Mr. and Mrs. E. W. Warren called at the A. O. Kramer home last Sabbath afternoon.

Mrs. R. N. Jensen is proud of that new washing machine. Sure enough, she brought the machine into the living room and as she already had a cracked window pane she brought the exhaust pipe through it out on the porch, and so did her washing by the warm stove and also dried the washing inside.

Mr. Marvin Jensen is busy these cold days fixing up a patent grind stone, run by the pump engine. He plans to have his ax sharp without so much hard work.

Well, this is about a Jensen news letter but when it is so cold people in the country do not create much news—at least that I can get hold of sitting by the stove.

Tuesday morning we have 4 above zero.

PeLee. A.J. Jensen, an immigrant from Denmark, and his wife, Lou, came to Texas from Kansas in 1909 and purchased land six miles east of Elgin. They deeded some land to the Seventh-Day Adventist Church for a parochial school and church and farmed the rest. They called the community PeLee, the Hebrew word for "wonderful," which came to Lou Jensen in a dream. Other families came, and PeLee became an Adventist colony where some of the best vegetables in Central Texas were grown. For over 30 years, Lou wrote a column in the *Elgin Courier* each week called the "PeLee News." In this column, she reported the community news and happenings, interpreted scripture, gave agricultural instructions, predicted the weather, and shared her philosophical views.

Six

WAR AND PEACE

Elgin's beginning in 1872 found the United States recovering from the Civil War. Peace seemed to have come at last to the country and to Texas. The schism of slavery was gone, but Reconstruction was painful. Elgin's growing population included veterans of Indian skirmishes, the Texas revolution, and the Confederate forces. War tales were shared on the street, in barbershops, and at other gatherings.

But more tales were added as the town progressed. People from Elgin served in the Texas militia, which was mobilized in domestic and border disputes; Elgin men volunteered for service in World War I, with one person killed. Some area people were displaced from homes and farms when the US Army built Camp Swift between Elgin and Bastrop in 1942. Men and women served in World War II, and families anguished when husbands and sons were prisoners of war or missing in action, which occurred in pursuit of that evasive thing—peace.

Patriotism has never been lacking in Elgin. Flags fly on holidays, bumper stickers on pickup trucks state, "Proud To Be An American," and children study Texas and US history in school and repeatedly pledge allegiance to the flag. Young people continue to enlist in the volunteer services of the nation.

F.S. Wade. Frederick Solvereign Wade came to Texas in 1857, taught school in Lee County, and moved to Elgin in 1900. In 1860, while visiting in Illinois, he was summoned to meet with a former acquaintance—president-elect Abraham Lincoln. Lincoln offered to pay Wade if he would influence Texas against secession from the Union. Wade informed Lincoln that Texas would join the Confederacy and he would support them. Wade returned to Texas, joined the Confederate army, was taken captive, and was held in prison at Elmira, New York. Stories say he walked home from Elmira at the end of the war. He was elected to the first Elgin City Council and was active with Confederate veterans in the Green Brigade Reunions held annually. Wade arranged the reunion to be in Elgin on June 23, 1925, but he died two weeks before it.

46th ANNUAL REUNION GREEN'S BRIGADE June 24, 1925 ELGIN TEX.

JAKE STANDIFER CAMP. Many veterans from the Texas Revolution, Indian skirmishes, and the Confederate army gathered on May 19, 1885, for a reunion headed by Jacob Standifer. Standifer, son of Elizabeth Standifer, fought at San Jacinto as well as in the Confederate army. He lived 2.5 miles southeast of Elgin on land he acquired for being in the Texas army; he died in 1901 at the age of 83.

TEXAS INFANTRY. Pictured fourth from the left in the back row, Mason Cole, of Elgin, was a member of Company E, 2nd Division of the Texas Infantry along the Rio Grande in 1917. These guardsmen were mobilized when Germany supported and encouraged Mexican raids into Texas. The US Army absorbed this company when World War I began.

LOYALTY PARADE. The United States declared war on Germany in April 1917, and Elgin expressed itself in a downtown Loyalty Parade that summer. Many Elginites sent sons to fight and defend the nation during this war.

MOBILE RECRUITING STATION. Different methods of recruiting were used to encourage young men to join the armed forces. Mobile stations appeared like this one from the US Army Medical Department, and posters were prevalent. One poster featured a young woman in a sailor suit saying, "Gee, I wish I were a man, I'd join the Navy now."

SOWELL BROTHERS.
Three sons of an Elgin
family were veterans of
World War I. Sam (left)
and Ellis (right) Sowell
joined the Navy in 1915
and served on the USS
Hopkins, a torpedo boat,
that swept the coasts
of North and South
America, guarding
against German
submarine attacks.
Their brother Adolph
was in the infantry
branch of the US Army.

DEE LEO PFEIFFER. Dee Pfeiffer is shown
here in his World War I uniform in
front of a flag. Dee and his brother Ollie
Clement both served their country well.
Ollie answered his call in the latter part
of his senior year in high school and was
in the 7th Battalion of the 165th Depot
Brigade. Both men returned to Elgin
and lived here the rest of their lives.

103

WORLD WAR I, ARMY AIR CORPS. From the Wright brothers' initial flight in 1903 until 1917, the United States waivered in acceptance of air power for military action. Finally, when World War I began, the military purchased land in Houston to train pilots for combat missions. Roy Rivers, pictured, is shown with his plane at Ellington Field in 1917.

HENRY LUNDGREN. Henry A. Lundgren, son of Emil Lundgren, was the only Elgin area soldier to die in World War I. He was killed in France, and his brother Edwin O. Lundgren, who was also fighting in France, went to where his body was buried. Edwin arranged to have it sent home and buried in the New Sweden Cemetery. The VFW post in Elgin is named in his honor.

NOVEMBER 11, 1918. Germany signed a treaty on November 11, 1918, to end World War I, and this celebration broke out in Elgin. Imagine the joy at the Oscar Davis house when son Clay was on the front porch telling the family goodbye, and as he was leaving to be shipped overseas, they heard the Oil Mill whistle blowing—the war had ended!

MEMORIAL TO VETERANS. The Henry A. Lundgren American Legion Post No. 295 applied for and obtained the pictured German 77-milimeter cannon, brought to America as ballast, and placed it in Veterans' Park following World War I. After necessary repairs, it was rededicated on May 30, 1983, as a memorial to World War I veterans and all veterans of this community.

CAMP SWIFT. Following the attack on Pearl Harbor on December 7, 1941, the contract to build the Bastrop County Training Camp was issued on January 19, 1942. This site had been chosen in 1940. The government condemned 52,162 acres of land between Elgin and Bastrop where there were 452 landowners. The people were given one month to vacate everything; their houses were eventually used as bombing targets. The contract for the camp required completion within 120 working days and was designed to accommodate 44,000 troops. The training camp was named Camp Swift after Eban Swift, a World War I commander and author. Swift was the largest training and transshipment camp in Texas. During World War II, it reached a maximum strength of 90,000 troops; it also housed 3,865 German prisoners.

SCRAP METAL DRIVE PARADE, 1942. In 1942, Americans got their first taste of recycling. They were encouraged to salvage tin cans, bottles, scrap metal of any type, and fats and cooking oils. Even the farmers were encouraged to do the following by the John Deere Company: "Sink a sub from your farm. Bring in your scrap." And the patriotic Elgin people came together for a parade and donated such.

RATIONING. Instituted in the spring of 1942, rationing was a system that provided everyone with the same amount of scarce goods. The system was designed to keep prices low and to make sure people had what they needed. Rationing stamps in limited numbers were issued, and one could only buy the items shown on this list with stamps plus money.

Rationed Items	Rationing Duration
Tires	January 1942 to December 1945
Cars	February 1942 to October 1945
Bicycles	July 1942 to September 1945
Gasoline	May 1942 to August 1945
Fuel Oil & Kerosene	October 1942 to August 1945
Solid Fuels	September 1943 to August 1945
Stoves	December 1942 to August 1945
Rubber Footwear	October 1942 to September 1945
Shoes	February 1943 to October 1945
Sugar	May 1942 to 1947
Coffee	November 1942 to July 1943
Processed Foods	March 1943 to August 1945
Meats, canned fish	March 1943 to November 1945
Cheese, canned milk, fats	March 1943 to November 1945
Typewriters	March 1942 to April 1944

CAPT. WILLIS POWELL CULP III. Elgin sent many young people to war. The two sons of the Powell Culp family were pilots; both were taken prisoners of war. W.P. Culp III, a pursuit pilot, was captured during the fall of Corregidor in 1942, survived the forced Bataan Death March, and spent the remainder of the war in Japanese prison camps. He returned to Texas after the war, died in 1972, and is buried in Arlington Cemetery.

JACK HAYS CULP. Jack and his mother are pictured on his 16th birthday. He flew a P-47 Thunderbolt, was shot down over Europe, and was a German prisoner until the war ended. He returned to Texas, reentered the service, and was a pilot in Korea and Vietnam. Major Culp was killed as a passenger in a corporate jet in Dallas in 1967 and is also buried in Arlington.

ELGIN USO. With its proximity to Camp Swift, Elgin operated a United Service Organization (USO) canteen from 1942 through 1946. The USO had been organized nationally to meet on-leave recreation needs for members of the armed forces. It focused on spiritual, religious, educational, and welfare needs of the men and women. A birthday party celebration is shown that was held in Elgin in 1944.

USO CIGARETTE GIRLS. Elginites Patricia Ricks Hendricks (left) and Mattie Bell Upchurch Smith (right) were favorites of unidentified soldiers as they were dressed in classic "cigarette girl" attire and sold cigarettes at the USO.

USO Girls, 1944. Local girls entered a contest for the title of Miss USO of Elgin. The winner was Joy Cole Fromme, pictured in the center of the first row with a rose in her hand.

Dance at Camp Swift. Despite a high enlistment rate in the US Army, African Americans were not treated equally. Racial tensions existed. At parades, church services, in transportation, and canteens, races were kept separate. African American soldiers were fighting alongside other US soldiers in the invasion of Europe, but they were separated at Camp Swift. Shown is a scene from an African American dance in 1944.

VICTORY GARDEN AT CAMP SWIFT. With rationing, the government encouraged people to plant Victory Gardens and grow their own vegetables and fruits. Nearly 20 million Americans answered the call as they planted gardens in backyards, empty lots, and even city rooftops—all in the name of patriotism. People were also encouraged to can their own vegetables and save the commercial canned goods for the troops.

GERMAN PRISONERS OF WAR. John Carter (left) managed the shoe repair shop at Camp Swift and worked some of the Germans soldiers captured from Rommel's elite Afrika Corps. At least 11 of the prisoners of war are buried on the Camp Swift grounds. After the war, the Camp Swift prisoners were sent to England for two years to help with cleanup before they were sent back to Germany.

NURSES. Several Elgin girls answered the call to become nurses and serve in the armed services. Lt. Pauline Speer Marzec Bostic (middle, on camel) finished nursing school in Austin prior to enlistment and is shown with two other unidentified nurses in front of the Sphinx in Egypt as they were waiting for the European invasion. Later, Bostic was in a medical group that talked a German commander into surrendering the town of Friedburg, Germany.

JACK WEBB. Capt. Jack Webb lost his leg below the knee when he stepped on a mine in France. Fellow soldiers carried him a long way to the medics. Jack always said his greatest fear was bleeding to death before he got medical help. Webb returned to Elgin and practiced law for over 40 years.

CLARENCE HUFF. In 1942, Clarence Huff was 17 years old and enlisted in the US Navy prior to graduation. He saw action in the Atlantic, North Africa, and the Pacific. Fifty years later, Elgin High seniors asked Clarence and several other World War II veterans to join in their commencement exercises where they were given honorary graduation diplomas—a fitting tribute to those who protected and served with honor!

LT. COL. ISABELLE GILLUM DUBAR. Soon after World War II began, Isabelle enlisted in the US Army as a dietitian. During her Army career, she was stationed on posts in the continental United States and in Japan; after the war, she served as dietitian in various veteran hospitals. She was discharged in 1965, having served in the armed forces for over 20 years.

DISMISSAL OF TROOPS. World War II ended in 1945, and Camp Swift closed in 1946. The overall dismissal pageantry is pictured with the flags flying, the 2nd Division marching, and spectators and buildings in the background. On March 11, 1946, Gen. Jonathan Wainwright is shown on the reviewing stand as the troops march by. Elgin mayor Buck Christian is shown third from the right in the first row. Camp Swift had been the training place for more than 90,000 troops. The most memorable group was the 10th Mountain Division with its pack mules. This division trained at Swift prior to being sent to the invasion of Italy and encountering the mountains. The closing of Camp Swift severely affected the economy of Elgin for many years.

SUPREME SACRIFICE. The flag-draped coffin of Pvt. Rudolph Eklund was returned home to Elgin by train after World War II and met by American Legion member Richard Green (in forefront) and other unidentified American Legion members. Eklund was taken prisoner in March 1942 and was in Japanese prison camps in Burma and Thailand, where he was forced to work on the Bridge on the River Kwai. He died in January 1944. Elgin lost many sons in this war, and some were buried abroad and others were brought home for burial. When a body arrived by train, Elgin followed the custom of sounding of the Oil Mill whistle and the fire siren. All stores closed their doors in tribute. The body was always accompanied by a military escort and was received by members of the American Legion and the Veterans of Foreign Wars.

DELK ODEN. Elgin High School has had two graduates finish service academies and serve their country. Maj. Gen. Delk Oden graduated from West Point in 1937 (shown in uniform), served in both World War II and Vietnam, and is buried at Arlington Cemetery.

ALBERT PAINE WILLIAMS. Williams graduated from Elgin High School in 1953 and from the US Naval Academy in 1957. He served in the Navy for five years and then obtained a doctorate degree from Tufts University in development economics. He worked for the Rand Corporation. He died in November 2000.

Seven

JUST REMINISCING

Elgin is the quintessential small Texas town that provokes individual memories through these pictures and stories. Times have changed, and memories grow. Nostalgia is widespread! People speak of Saturday nights on Upchurch Corner, hamburgers at the Silver Spot, special trains to football games, serials at the Eltex on Saturday afternoons, telephone party lines, and Dr. Fleming making house calls.

Yet today, air-conditioning is enjoyed in homes, businesses, and schools; smart phones are helpful tools for keeping in touch; school textbooks are on computers; every high school student drives a car; and there are huge supermarkets.

Who does not remember a beautiful wedding or some of Elgin's festivals or listening to talented musicians? Childhood toys change with each generation, and cars no longer crowd Main Street on Saturdays. Never again will residents go to Joe Simon's store, get a Coke float at Upchurch Drug, fill their car with Sinclair gasoline at Arbuckle Oil, or spend $1 at Mikulencak Variety Store. Residents are very fortunate to have a legacy of a small town.

Elgin has been blessed in its 140-year history, as it has progressed from a watering spot for the railroad to a vibrant community that celebrates individuality. May memories and happenings of the people of Elgin, Texas, be kept alive.

A FAMILY OUTING. All family members always enjoyed a fishing trip to the Colorado River, and a huge catch of fish made it more appreciated. Carrie and Joe Dildy and son Joseph (on the left) and Leslie and Lovie Fisher with children James and Cecil (on the right) had such a trip in 1917. They took pictures to show that the fish did not get away!

"LOOK AT ME!" William Howard Rivers III was the envy of every child in Elgin in 1927. Shown here in front of the bank that his grandfather founded, "Little Howard" is driving his first car. His parents had been to New York and purchased this for him at F.A.O. Schwarz, the renowned toy store.

JACK WEBB'S FIRST BIRTHDAY PARTY. Birthday parties have always been celebrated. Jack was born in 1922, and evidently, his mother made his first party quite a celebration. However, the only baby identified is Bernhart Smith, second from the left in the top row with his mother's hands visible.

BIRTHDAY PARTY IN THE 1950s. Themes for birthday parties progressed as the town grew. Alice Martin Davis had quite a celebration for her seventh birthday. Pictured are Jon Lynn Ray, Brownie Cashion, Karin Lundgren, Ronald Lowther, Floyd Johnson, Patricia Larson, Charles Boettcher, Clifford Pate, Lynn Kiker, Jimmy Schanhals, Fred Gustafson, Ed Davis, Tina Boettcher, Joy Bingham, Carol Ann Prewitt, Carol Burke, Alice Davis, Judy Davis, and Arthur Schroeder Jr.

SWEDISH WEDDING PARTY. Walter Lind and Amy Smith (in the center of the first row) were married in 1914 in the Kimbro Evangelical Free Church. Weddings were quite elaborate celebrations for the Swedish population around Elgin. Walter worked at the Kimbro store and farmed, and Amy raised their three children, Maydell, Leslie, and June. They left the farm in their later years and moved to Austin.

MR. AND MRS. ARTHUR SCHROEDER. Arthur Schroeder and Bertha Klaus married in an impressive Lutheran ceremony on December 17, 1923. Both the bride and groom were from large German families and the couple continued living in the area all of their lives. Sons and grandchildren of this family today continue with the inherited German work ethic.

MAY FETE QUEEN, 1919. The Elgin schools presented several salutes to spring through the years. Zelma Prewitt McCall, pictured, was queen of the May Fete in 1919. Two thousand people witnessed the pageantry at the ballpark, as the grand march was lead by Uncle Sam (Emmet Carter) and Miss Columbia (Margaret McCullough). The different classes honored the queen with dances, drills, and marches in elaborate and appropriate costumes.

WASHINGTON HIGH HOMECOMING ROYALTY. Homecoming has always been a special time for schools. The members of this Washington High Homecoming Court in 1943 are unidentified. World War II was in progress, and many of the male students were already fighting in foreign lands.

DIEZ Y SEIS CELEBRATION. Mexico declared its independence from Spain on September 16, 1810, and people of Hispanic background celebrate this date every year. Elgin, since 1917, has looked forward to this annual celebration of food, music, and dancing. Queen Katherine Perez Slay is shown (middle) as she enters with her court of unidentified persons in 1950.

HARVEST FESTIVAL. During the 1940s and 1950s, Elgin students looked forward to the Harvest Festival (a Halloween carnival) in late October. This royal court of 1949 included, from left to right, (first row) Betty Carol Johnson, Anita Holmes, Glenda Lax, and Shirlene Peterson; (second row) Don Thormahlen, Clyde Lane, king L.C. Fisher, queen Laverne Kylberg, Karl Engeling, and Bobby Reynolds.

ELGIN DANCE BAND. Without synthesizers or percussion, local musicians performed. This local band in 1952 was composed of Bill Rivers, trumpet; Albert Paine Williams, saxophone; Donald Gustafson, alto saxophone, Louis "Zoom" Hashem, guitar; Jimmy Lundgren, piano; and Bill Henry, announcer.

PAUL OCHOA'S RHYTHM BOYS. Paul Ochoa worked for Paul Farris in the day and led his band at night in Mexican music for festivals and dances. Together with unidentified band members, Paul and his two children are recognized as follows: son Lambert (child), daughter Lolita (middle row, second from right), and Paul (middle row, right). It is almost as though one can hear the strains of "El Rancho Grande" by just looking at the picture.

CHILDREN CELEBRATE. Patricia Webb and Mark Gibbons participated in the Tiny Tot Review of a Yamboree Festival in the 1950s. Children who participated in such events have grown into accomplished adults because of the teaching and nurturing of parents who showed pride in their children. It is doubtful that Martha and George Washington were ever as attractive as Patricia and Mark!

ICE CREAM CONES. Cousins enjoy ice cream cones in a booth at Upchurch Drug in the 1950s. Pictured from left to right, Mike Fisher, Dale Dildy, Vernon Glenn Smith, and Lee Dildy make Diane Dildy stand as they pose and lick at the same time. Upchurch was the place in town where one could eat a sandwich; drink a malt; purchase newspapers, magazines, perfume, costume jewelry, cosmetics, pottery, crystal, and fine china; get advice on prescriptions; and even play pinball games.

JUDGE AND MRS. C.W. WEBB. Charles W. Webb and Emma Stulken Webb were both lawyers and were central figures in Elgin from 1900 until the 1980s. Judge Webb, as he was known, began practicing law in Elgin in 1900. He had a great gift of writing and was a friend to all people, regardless of color or station in life. Emma Stulken came to Elgin as a schoolteacher and soon married the widowed Judge Webb. She distinguished herself by entering the University of Texas Law School and was the first female editor of the *UT Law Review*. Emma Webb's stately demeanor commanded respect in any situation she was involved in. There would be very little documented history or pictures of Elgin if the Webbs had not gathered and saved important papers and pictures.

DAVIS & SCHANHALS. Syd Davis and Otis Schanhals opened a new Pontiac agency and service station in June 1948. Pictured at this event are, from left to right, (first row) Judy Davis, Sydna Davis Arbuckle, and Jim Schanhals; (second row): Paul G. Lundgren, Nell Davis, Ruth Schanhals, Otis Schanhals, Syd Davis, and Lyle Talley. In 2012, Pontiac automobiles, Humble gasoline, Southwest Conference football radio broadcasts, and the cherished people in the second row exist only in memories.

THREE OF US. Sydna Arbuckle (left), Ann Helgeson (center), and Judy Davis (right) have learned much about our town in compiling this volume. Hope you discovered some interesting things also!

There are over 4,000 more Elgin photos at the **Elgin Depot Museum**

PO Box 1234 Elgin, TX 78621
elgindepot@gmail.com

museum open Tues-Sun 2-5 pm

ELGIN DEPOT MUSEUM. Volumes of local photographs are at the Elgin Depot Museum. Come and see them!

Visit us at
arcadiapublishing.com

CPSIA information can be obtained
at www.ICGtesting.com
Printed in the USA
LVHW101302030521
686338LV00006B/40